WHEN THEY KILL A PRESIDENT

SPECIAL EDITION

WHEN THEY KILL A PRESIDENT

SPECIAL EDITION

BY

ROGER DEAN CRAIG

When They Kill a President: Special Edition. Copyright © 2021 by Steve Cameron. All rights reserved. Printed in the United States of America. No part of this book may be reproduced, distributed, or transmitted in any form or by any means, including photocopying, recording, or other electronic or mechanical methods, without the prior written permission of the publisher, except in the case of brief quotations embodied in critical reviews and certain other noncommercial uses permitted by United States of America copyright law.

The events in this book are from Roger Dean Craig's memories, and from Roger Dean Craig's perspective, and may not be the memories, or perspectives of other individuals named in this book.

Published by Steve Cameron Productions
Cover and book design by Steve Cameron

Manuscript originally written by Roger D. Craig in 1971, and edited by Rita Musgrove. Special Edition edited by Steve Cameron.

stevecameronproductions.com

"We are not afraid to entrust the American people with unpleasant facts, foreign ideas, alien philosophies, and competitive values. For a nation that is afraid to let its people judge the truth and falsehood in an open market is a nation that is afraid of its people."

—John Fitzgerald Kennedy

May 29, 1917 – November 22, 1963

INTRODUCTION

When They Kill a President was originally written in 1971 as an unpublished manuscript by Roger Dean Craig, a decorated Dallas Deputy Sheriff who won 'Officer of the Year' for Dallas County in 1960 for outstanding performance in the line of duty. This new 2021 Special Edition of Craig's manuscript documents his eyewitness account of the assassination of President John F. Kennedy, his investigation in Dealey Plaza after it occurred, and the massive cover up that followed.

Among the many things that Craig witnessed, was a man identical to Lee Harvey Oswald run from the Texas School Book Depository and get picked up by a light-colored Nash Rambler station wagon minutes after Kennedy was shot. He was also present during the discovery of a 7.65 Mauser rifle found on the 6th-floor of the depository — a completely different rifle than the one entered into evidence as being the only weapon used to shoot at President Kennedy's motorcade.

In April of 1964, Roger Craig testified as a Key Witness before the Warren Commission. However, according to Craig, portions of his testimony were changed, and other parts completely omitted from the commission's final report.

Craig was also pressured by his boss, Sheriff Bill Decker, to keep quiet about what he witnessed in the days and years after the assassination. And on July 4, 1967, Sheriff Decker fired Roger Craig, because he suspected his deputy was cooperating with New Orleans District Attorney Jim Garrison, who had recently charged Clay LaVerne Shaw for participating in a conspiracy to kill Kennedy. Craig would later testify as a Key Witness for Garrison's trial of Shaw on February 14, 1969.

After numerous attempts were made on his life, which began in 1967 soon after his first meeting with Jim Garrison, Roger Craig was found shot to death under very mysterious circumstances on May 15, 1975, just days before a scheduled in-person interview that he was supposed to have with photo expert Robert Groden, who at the time was working for Congressman Thomas H. Downing of Virginia. Downing was in the early stages of reopening the investigation into President Kennedy's murder, and had sent Groden to Dallas to interview Craig about what he knew. Downing's investigation later led to the formation of the House Select Committee on Assassinations in 1976. And according to Robert Groden, Roger Craig would have been called as a Key Witness before their committee. But sadly, like many others leading up to Downing's HSCA hearings, he died before he ever had the chance to testify.

This first-hand account of what took place in Dallas on November 22, 1963, proves not only that there was a vast conspiracy to kill John F. Kennedy, but it also examines how costly telling the truth could be for an eyewitness like Roger Craig, who threatened to expose the lies of the official narrative surrounding the assassination of the 35th President of the United States.

Steve Cameron

Author of *The Deputy Interviews: The True Story of J.F.K. Assassination Witness, and Former Dallas Deputy Sheriff, Roger Dean Craig.*

WHEN THEY KILL A PRESIDENT

SPECIAL EDITON

CHAPTER 1

Our president John Kennedy went down to Dallas town Where

the hired assassins waited and there they shot him down

Because he dreamed of peace and plenty and he talked it

'round His dream goes marching on

The Dallas County Court House at 505 Main Street was indeed a unique place to come to hear what was WRONG with John F. Kennedy and his policies as President of these United States.

This building housed the elite troops of the Dallas County Sheriff's Department (of which I was one), who, with blind obedience, followed the orders of their Great White Father: Bill Decker, Sheriff of Dallas County.

From these elite troops came the most bitter verbal attacks on President Kennedy. They spoke very strongly against his policies concerning the Bay of Pigs incident and the Cuban Missile crisis. They seemed to resent very much the fact that President Kennedy was a Catholic. I do not know why this was such a critical issue with many of the deputies but they did seem to hold this against President Kennedy.

The concession stand in the lobby of the court house was the best place to get into a discussion concerning the President. The old man who ran the stand evidenced a particular hatred for President Kennedy. He seemed to go out of his way to drag anyone who came by his stand into a discussion about the President. His name is J. C. Kiser.

He was a little man with a short mustache and glasses that he wore right on the end of his nose. He was a particularly good friend of Sheriff Decker, and he held the concession in the lobby for many years. Like Decker, he was unopposed when his lease came up for renewal. It was common knowledge that Bill Decker made it possible for him to remain there as long as he wished. This sick little man not only had a deep hatred for John F. Kennedy, he also hated the black people, even those who spent their money at his stand. He would often curse them as they walked away after making a purchase from him. He flatly refused to make telephone change for them even though he would be simultaneously making change for a white person.

This little man was a typical example of the atmosphere that lingered in this building that housed law and order in Dallas County.

Many of the deputies had a dislike for the President—some more so than others. However, there were those who would not degrade themselves by taking verbal punches at our President. One of these was Hiram Ingram. Although devoted to Bill Decker, he was also a good friend of mine. We often discussed the political debates that took place in the lobby. Hiram had a great dislike for this sick little man who seemed to lead the attack on the President. He also had little respect for the deputies, attorneys and court house employees who tolerated or even agreed with this philosophy of attacking John F. Kennedy.

Hiram Ingram was a small man—in stature. He was always ready with a friendly smile and greeting. He began his association with the County during the Bonnie and Clyde era—when he was an ambulance driver and inside employee at a local funeral home. In fact, Hiram prepared Bonnie and Clyde for burial after they were brought back to Dallas from the ambush in Louisiana.

Hiram and I were very close—one of those friendships which develops when some people first meet. I had known Hiram for about four years at the time of the assassination. He was working in the Civil Division and shortly after November 22, 1963 he had a heart attack. When he returned to work Decker put him on the Bond Desk, where I would later be and work closely with Hiram. I worked the day shift one month and the evening shift the following month. Hiram worked only evenings. So every other month we worked together. This gave us time to talk and discuss the events in Dallas and even the Sheriff's Office itself. The Department was not well organized.

To clear some of the bonds and bondsmen we would have to call Decker at home—no matter what time of the day or night—for his approval or any decision. This applied only to certain bondsmen. Decker had his chosen few who were not questioned. Hiram was a very dependable employee and should not have had to clear the minor decisions with our Great White Father, Bill Decker.

As the months passed and Hiram and I worked together we built a mutual respect for each other. When Decker fired me on July 4, 1967 Hiram was infuriated but, like any employee of Decker's, he couldn't say anything in my defense for fear of having his employment cut short or his reputation ruined. One of Decker's favorite past times was ruining reputations.

Our friendship did not end with my termination. We continued to talk from time to time and Hiram was very helpful when Penn Jones wanted information concerning records at the Sheriff's office. However, in March of 1968 Hiram explained to me that information was getting more difficult to get for some reason. Fortunately, by this time I had already supplied Penn Jones and Bill Boxley (investigator for Jim Garrison) with much information from Hiram.

About two weeks later, near the end of March 1968, I heard that Hiram had fallen at home and broken his hip and was in the hospital. I went to see my good buddy to cheer him up and received the shock of my life. Hiram was under oxygen and could not have any visitors. Three days later he was dead—of cancer. He had been working just prior to the fall. I think that we owe a debt of gratitude to this great man who, in his own quiet way, helped us all so much.

Thus . . . we have the atmosphere that was to greet the President of the United States upon his arrival in Dallas. However, things were to get even worse before he arrived.

The battle ground had been picked and the UNwelcome mat was out for President Kennedy. Unknown to most of us, the rest of the plan was being completed. The patsy had been chosen and placed in the building across from the court house—where he could not deny his presence after it was all over. This was done with the apparent approval and certainly with the knowledge of our co-workers, the F.B.I., since they later admitted that they knew Lee Harvey Oswald was employed at the School Book Depository Building located on the corner of Elm Street and Houston Street across from the Sheriff's Office.

The security had been arranged by the Secret Service and the Dallas Police—our boys in blue. The final touch was put on by Sheriff James Eric (Bill) Decker. On the morning of November 22, 1963, the patrolmen in the districts which make up the Dallas County Sheriff's Patrol Division were left in the field, ignorant of what was going on in the downtown area, which was just as well. Decker was not going to LET them do anything anyway.

About 10:30 a.m. November 22, 1963, Bill Decker called into his office what I will refer to as his street people—plain-clothes men, detectives and warrant men, myself included—and told us that President Kennedy was coming to Dallas and that the motorcade would come down Main Street. He then advised us that we were to stand out in front of the building, 505 Main Street and represent the Sheriff's Office. We were to take no part whatsoever in the security of that motorcade. (Why, James Eric?) So . . . the stage had been set, all the pawns were in place, the security had been withdrawn from that one vulnerable location. Come John F. Kennedy, come to Elm and Houston Streets in Dallas, Texas and take your place in history!

The time was 12:15 p.m. I was standing in front of the court house at 505 Main Street. Deputy Sheriff Jim Ramsey was standing behind me. We were waiting for the President of the United States. I had a feeling of pride that I was going to be not more than four feet from the President but deep inside something kept gnawing at me. I said to Jim Ramsey, "He's late." Jim's reply stunned me. He said, "Maybe somebody will shoot the son of a bitch." Then I realized the crowd was hostile. The men about me felt that they were forced to acknowledge his presence. Although he was the President, they were making statements like, "Why does he have to come to Dallas?"

Something else was bothering me . . . being a trained officer, I always looked for anything which might be amiss about any situation with which I was confronted. Suddenly I knew what was wrong. There were no officers guarding the intersections or controlling the crowd. My mind flashed back to the meeting in Decker's office that morning, then back to the lack of security in this area.

Suddenly the motorcade approached and President Kennedy was smiling and waving and for a moment I relaxed and fell into the happy mood the President was displaying. The car turned the corner onto Houston Street. I was still looking at the rest of the people in the party. I was soon to be shocked back into reality. The President had passed and was turning west on Elm Street . . . as if there were no people, no cars, the only thing in my world at that moment was a rifle shot! I bolted toward Houston Street. I was fifteen steps from the corner— before I reached it two more shots had been fired. Telling myself that it wasn't true and at the same time knowing that it was, I continued to run. I ran across Houston Street and beside the pond, which is on the west side of Houston. I pushed a man out of my way and he fell into the pond. I ran down the grass between Main and Elm. People were lying all over the ground. I thought, "My God, they've killed a woman and child," who were lying beside the gutter on the South side of Elm Street. I checked them and they were alright. I saw a Dallas Police Officer run up the grassy knoll and go behind the picket fence near the railroad yards. I followed and behind the fence was complete confusion and hysteria.

I began to question people when I noticed a woman in her early thirties attempting to drive out of the parking lot. She was in a brown 1962 or 1963 Chevrolet. I stopped her, identified myself and placed her under arrest. She told me that she had to leave and I said, "Lady, you're not going anywhere." I turned her over to Deputy Sheriff C. I. (Lummy) Lewis and told him the circumstances of the arrest. Officer Lewis told me that he would take her to Sheriff Decker and take care of her car.

The parking lot behind the picket fence was of little importance to most of the investigators at the scene except that the shots were thought to have come from there.

Let us examine this parking lot. It was leased by Deputy Sheriff B. D. Gossett. He in turn rented parking space by the month to the deputies who worked in the court house, except for official vehicles. I rented one of these spaces from Gossett when I was a dispatcher working days or evenings. I paid Gossett $3.00 per month and was given a key to the lot. An interesting point is that the lot had an iron bar across the only entrance and exit (which were the same). The bar had a chain and lock on it. The only people having access to it were deputies with keys. Point: how did the woman gain access and, what is more important, who was she and why did she have to leave?

This was to be the beginning of the never-ending cover up. Had I known then what I know now, I would have personally questioned the woman and impounded and searched her car. I had no way of knowing that an officer, with whom I had worked for four years, was capable of losing a thirty-year-old woman and a three-thousand-pound automobile. To this day Officer Lewis does not know who she was, where she came from or what happened to her. Strange!

Meanwhile, back at the parking lot, I continued to help the Dallas Officers restore order. When things were somewhat calmer, I began to question the people who were standing at the top of the grassy knoll, asking if anyone had seen anything strange or unusual before or during the President's fatal turn onto Elm Street.

Several people indicated to me that they thought the shots came from the area of the grassy knoll or behind the picket fence. My next reliable witness came forward in the form of Mr. Arnold Rowland. Mr. Rowland and his wife were standing at the top of the grassy knoll on the north side of Elm Street. Arnold Rowland began telling me his account of what he saw before the assassination. He said approximately fifteen minutes before President Kennedy arrived, he was looking around and something caught his eye. It was a white man standing by the 6th floor window of the Texas School Book Depository Building in the southeast corner, holding a rifle equipped with a telescopic sight and in the southwest corner of the sixth floor was a colored male pacing back and forth. Needless to say, I was astounded by his statement. I asked Mr. Rowland why he had not reported this incident before and he told me that he thought they were secret service agents—an obvious conclusion for a layman. Rowland continued. He told me that he looked back at the sixth floor a few minutes later and the man with the rifle was gone so he dismissed it from his mind.

I was writing all this down in my notebook and when I finished, I advised Mr. and Mrs. Rowland that I would have to detain them for a statement. I had started toward the Sheriff's Office with them when lo and behold I was approached by Officer C. L. (Lummy) Lewis, who asked me "What ya got"—a favorite expression of most investigators with Bill Decker. I explained the situation to him and told him of Rowland's account. Being the Good Samaritan he was, Officer Lewis offered to take the Rowlands off my hands and get their statements. This worked out a little better than my first arrest. The Warren Commission decided not to accept Arnold Rowland's story but at least they did not lose them. Hang in there, Lummy!

The time was approximately 12:40 p.m. I had just turned the Rowlands over to Lummy Lewis when I met E. R. (Buddy) Walthers, a small man with a very arrogant manner. He was, without a doubt, Decker's favorite pupil. He wore dark-rimmed glasses and a small-brimmed hat because effecting them meant that he would resemble Bill Decker. Walthers had worked for the Yellow Cab Company of Dallas before coming to the Sheriff's Office, about a year before I began working there. His termination from the cab company was the result of several shortages of money. He came to the Sheriff's Department as a patrolman but because of his close connection with Justice of the Peace Bill Richburg—one of Decker's closest allies—Buddy soon was promoted to detective. He had absolutely no ability as a law enforcement officer. However, he was fast climbing the ladder of success by lying to Decker and squealing on his fellow officers.

Walthers' ambition was to become Sheriff of Dallas County and he would do anything or anybody to reach that goal. It was very clear Buddy enjoyed more job security with Decker than anyone else did. Decker carried him for years by breaking a case for him or taking a case which had been broken by another officer and putting Walthers' name on the arrest sheet. Soon after he was promoted to detective, he became intimate with such people as W. O. Bankston, the flamboyant Oldsmobile dealer in Dallas who furnished Decker with a new Fire Engine Red Olds every year and who was arrested several times for Driving while Intoxicated but never served any jail time.

Buddy's acquaintances also included several independent oil operators throughout Texas, several anti-Castro Cubans and many underworld characters—especially women! He was frequently crashing parties which were given by wealthy friends of Decker's—of course while he was on duty. He often became drunk and belligerent at these parties and at one point, when asked to leave, he threatened to pull his gun on the host. This information can be verified by Billy Courson, who was Buddy's partner at that time.

Walthers hit the big time when, in 1961, two Federal Narcotics Agents came to Decker's office with charges that Buddy was growing marijuana in the back yard of his home at 2527 Boyd Street in the Oak Cliff section of Dallas. This could be considered conduct unbecoming to a police officer—but not for Buddy! After a secret meeting between the Federal Agents, Decker and Buddy, the matter was dropped and—needless to say—covered up, thus enabling Buddy to continue his career as Decker's Representative of Law and Order in Dallas County.

However, the Dallas Police began receiving complaints that Buddy was shaking down underworld characters for loot taken in several burglaries and selling the stuff himself. After several reports the Dallas Police began to investigate and, finally, obtained a search warrant for Buddy's home. Their BIG mistake was securing the warrant from Judge Richburg—which was bad enough—but Buddy's wife also worked for Richburg and this made matters worse. Strangely enough, they did not find anything. However, a few weeks later they were a little more careful and made a surprise visit to Buddy's home, where they, indeed, recovered such things as toasters, clothing and various items—just as their informers had said. It would seem they had him this time, wouldn't it? But not so. Buddy explained that he had recovered the merchandise from where it had been hidden and had not had time to make a report on them and turn them in to the Property Room! The Dallas Police didn't buy this story but the pressure was again brought to bear by our

Protector, Bill Decker, and the Dallas Police were left out in the cold— no charges filed! They were certainly furious but what could they do? If WE as citizens cannot fight the Establishment, how can the Establishment fight the Establishment?

It was clear in my mind, and if the people with whom I worked could talk, I am sure they would agree that Buddy had a powerful hold on Decker. I base this on the fact that Buddy's popularity with Decker greatly increased after the assassination. Buddy was a chronic liar—he was always telling Decker things he thought were happening in the County which he was checking on. Things which he was not doing. He also told Decker that he was in the theater when Oswald was captured and that he, in fact, helped the Dallas Police. This was completely untrue. Buddy never entered the Texas Theater—his partner, Bill Courson, did.

Buddy also told Decker about a family of anti-Castro Cubans living in the Oak Cliff area and said that he was watching them. This part may have been true because we received the same information from the Dallas Police Intelligence Division. But one day Buddy made a visit to the house in Oak Cliff and when the Police and Sheriff's Deputies went to question them a few days later, they were gone. Did Buddy warn them? After all, he was very, very close to Jack Ruby. In fact, every time Buddy was in trouble with one of Jack Ruby's employees—especially Nancy Perrin Rich—Decker would send Buddy to straighten things out and put Nancy in her place—with the help of Judge Richburg. Touching Jack Ruby was a no-no!

There were many other things which made Buddy suspect as a not-so- law abiding lawman, such as the swimming pool he built in his back yard (on his salary?). The concrete was furnished by a local contractor free of charge. Buddy used many pills he carried in the trunk of his unmarked squad car for trading with certain underworld characters—pills for information. I learned from what I consider a reliable source that these pills had been confiscated (although no reports were made nor the pills turned in). Most of those involved in this exchange were women. It would seem that Buddy Walthers could not be terminated from the Sheriff's Department, no matter what.

One incident in 1966 which would have resulted in the firing of any other deputy occurred when Buddy was sent to Nevada to transfer a suspect wanted in Dallas. It seemed Buddy was given a certain amount of travel money which he lost at the gambling table in Las Vegas. Broke and in trouble, Buddy called none other than W. O. Bankston, who wired him enough money to bring his prisoner back to Dallas. Many times I wondered who was REALLY Sheriff but Buddy was about to reach the end of his rope.

In late 1968, when the Clay Shaw trial was being prepared, there was talk of bringing Buddy to New Orleans to testify. Well, that was a blow to the power which ruled Dallas. They could not have this half-wit on the witness stand. When the word reached Dallas, Decker was working on a double-murder which occurred in his county and had a lead on the suspect in January of 1969. The Shaw trial was scheduled for February and Decker sent

Buddy and his partner, Alvin Maddox (who was about as efficient as a nutty professor), to a motel on Samuell Boulevard in Dallas to question a Walter Cherry about the killings. Cherry was an escaped convict and a suspect in the double-murder. Decker sent them to talk to Cherry without a warrant. When they entered the room at the motel Buddy was shot dead and Maddox wounded in the FOOT. Coincidence? Maybe! At any rate Buddy had been silenced. One more point for Dallas!

Back to November 22, 1963. As I have earlier stated, the time was approximately 12:40 p.m. when I ran into Buddy Walthers. The traffic was very heavy as Patrolman Baker (assigned to Elm and Houston Streets) had left his post, allowing the traffic to travel west on Elm Street. As we were scanning the curb, I heard a shrill whistle coming from the north side of Elm Street. I turned and saw a white male in his twenties running down the grassy knoll from the direction of the Texas School Book Depository Building. A light green Rambler station wagon was coming slowly west on Elm Street. The driver of the station wagon was a husky looking Latin, with dark wavy hair, wearing a tan wind breaker type jacket. He was looking up at the man running toward him. He pulled over to the north curb and picked up the man coming down the hill. I tried to cross Elm Street to stop them and find out who they were. The traffic was too heavy and I was unable to reach them. They drove away going west on Elm Street.

In addition to noting that these two men were in an obvious hurry, I realized they were the only ones not running TO the scene. Everyone else was running to see whatever might be seen. The suspect, as I will refer to him, who ran down the grassy knoll was wearing faded blue trousers and a long-sleeved work shirt made of some type of grainy material. This will become very important to me later on and very embarrassing to the authorities (F.B.I., Dallas Police and Warren Commission). I thought the incident concerning the two men and the Rambler Station Wagon important enough to bring it to the attention of the authorities at the command post at Elm and Houston.

I ran to the front of the Texas School Book Depository where I asked for anyone involved in the investigation. There was a man standing on the steps of the Book Depository Building and he turned to me and said, "I'm with the Secret Service." This man was about 40 years old, sandy-haired with a distinct cleft in his chin. He was well-dressed in a gray business suit. I was naive enough at the time to believe that the only people there were actually officers—after all, this was the command post. I gave him the information. He showed little interest in the persons leaving. However, he seemed extremely interested in the description of the Rambler. This was the only part of my statement which he wrote down in his little pad he was holding. Point: Mrs. Ruth Paine, the woman Marina Oswald lived with in Irving, Texas, owned a Rambler station wagon, at that time, of this same color.

CHAPTER 2

From the book depository and of course that grassy knoll

And the Dal Tex building's shooter fulfilled his deadly role

The noon day sun was witness as they took their awful toll

His dream goes marching on

I learned nothing of this "Secret Service Agent's" identity until December 22, 1967 while we were living in New Orleans. The television was on as I came home from work one night and there on the screen was a picture of this man. I did not know what it was all about until my wife told me that Jim Garrison had charged him with being a part of the assassination plot. I called Jim Garrison then and told him that this was the man I had seen in Dallas on November 22, 1963. Jim then sent one of his investigators to see me with a better picture which I identified. I then learned that this man's name was Edgar Eugene Bradley. It was a relief to me to know his name for I had been bothered by the fact that I had failed to get his name when he had told me he was a Secret Service Agent and I had given him my information. On the night of the assassination when I had come home and discussed the day with my wife I had, of course, told her of this encounter and my failure to get his name.

As I finished talking with the Agent, I was confronted by the High Priest of Dallas County Politics, Field Marshal Bill Decker. Decker had, apparently, been standing directly behind me and had overheard what I was saying. He called me aside and informed me that the suspect had already left the scene. (How did you know, James Eric? You had just arrived.) Decker then told me to help them (the police) search the Book Depository Building. Decker turned toward his office across the street, then suddenly stopped, looked at me and said "Somebody better take charge of this investigation." Then he continued walking slowly toward his office, indicating that it was not going to be him.

When I entered the Book Depository Building, I was joined by Deputy Sheriffs Eugene Boone and Luke Mooney. We went up the stairs directly to the sixth floor. The room was very dark and a thick layer of dust seemed to cover everything. We went to the south side of the building, since this was the street side and seemed the most logical place to start.

Luke Mooney and I reached the southeast corner at the same time. We immediately found three rifle cartridges laying in such a way that they looked as though they had been carefully and deliberately placed there— in plain sight on the floor to the right of the southeast corner window. Mooney and I examined the cartridges very carefully and remarked how close together they were. The three of them were no more than one inch apart and all were facing in the same direction, a feat very difficult to achieve with a bolt action rifle—or any rifle for that matter. One cartridge drew our particular attention. It was crimped on the end which would have held the slug. It had not been stepped on but merely crimped over on one small portion of the rim. The rest of that end was perfectly round.

Laying on the floor to the left of the same window was a small brown paper lunch bag containing some well cleaned chicken bones. I called across the room and summoned the Dallas Police I.D. man, Lt. Day. When he arrived with his camera Mooney and I left the window and started our search of the rest of the sixth floor.

We were told by Dallas Police to look for a rifle—something I had already concluded might be there since the cartridges found were, apparently, from a rifle. I was nearing the northwest corner of the sixth floor when Deputy Eugene Boone called out, "here it is." I was about eight feet from Boone, who was standing next to a stack of cardboard boxes. The boxes were stacked so that there was no opening between them except at the top. Looking over the top and down the opening I saw a rifle with a telescopic sight laying on the floor with the bolt facing upward. At this time Boone and I were joined by Lt. Day of the Dallas Police Department and Dallas Homicide Captain, Will Fritz. The rifle was retrieved by Lt. Day, who activated the bolt, ejecting one live round of ammunition which fell to the floor.

Lt. Day inspected the rifle briefly, then handed it to Capt. Fritz who had a puzzled look on his face. Seymour Weitzman, a deputy constable, was standing beside me at the time. Weitzman was an expert on weapons. He had been in the sporting goods business for many years and was familiar with all domestic and foreign weapons. Capt. Fritz asked if anyone knew what kind of rifle it was.

Weitzman asked to see it. After a close examination (much longer than Fritz or Day's examination) Weitzman declared that it was a 7.65 German Mauser. Fritz agreed with him. Apparently, someone at the Dallas Police Department also loses things but, at least, they are more conscientious. They did replace it— even if the replacement was made in a different country. (See Warren Report for Italian Mannlicher-Carcano 6.5 Caliber).

At that exact moment an unknown Dallas police officer came running up the stairs and advised Capt. Fritz that a Dallas policeman had been shot in the Oak Cliff area. I instinctively looked at my watch. The time was 1:06 p.m. A token force of uniformed officers was left to keep the sixth floor secure and Fritz, Day, Boone, Mooney, Weitzman and I left the building.

On my way back to the Sheriff's Office I was nearly run down several times by Dallas Police cars racing to the scene of the shooting of a fellow officer. There were more police units at the J. D. Tippit shooting than there were at President John F. Kennedy's assassination.

Tippit had been instructed to patrol the Oak Cliff area along with Dallas Police Unit #87 at 12:45 p.m. by the dispatcher. Unit #87 immediately left Oak Cliff and went to the triple underpass, leaving Tippit alone. Why? At 12:54 p.m., J. D. Tippit, Dallas Police Unit #78, gave his location as Lancaster Blvd., and Eighth St., some ten blocks from the place where he was to be killed. The Dallas dispatcher called Tippit at 1:04 p.m. and received no answer. He continued to call three times and there was still no reply. Comparing this time with the time I received news of the shooting of the police officer at 1:06 p.m., it is fair to assume Tippit was dead or being killed between 1:04 and 1:06 p.m. This is also corroborated by the eye witnesses at the Tippit killing, who said he was shot between 1:05 and 1:08 p.m.

According to Officer Baker, Dallas Police, he talked to Oswald at 12:35 p.m. in the lunch room of the Texas School Book Depository. This would give Oswald 30 minutes or less to finish his coke, leave the building, walk four blocks east on Elm Street, catch a bus and ride it back west in heavy traffic for two blocks, get off the bus and walk two more blocks west and turn south on Lamar Street, walk four blocks and have a conversation with a cab driver and a woman over the use of Whaley's (the cab driver) cab, get into the cab and ride to 500 North Beckley Street, get out and walk to 1026 North Beckley where his (Oswald's) room was located, pick up something (?); and if that is not enough, Earlene Roberts, the housekeeper where Oswald lived, testified that at 1:05 p.m. Oswald was waiting for a bus in front of his rooming house and finally, to make him the fastest man on Earth, he walked to East Tenth Street and Patton Street, several blocks away and killed J. D. Tippit between 1:05 and 1:08 p.m. If he had not been arrested when he was, it is my belief that Earl Warren and his Commission would have had Lee Harvey Oswald eating dinner in Havana!

I was convinced on November 22, 1963, and I am still sure, that the man entering the Rambler station wagon was Lee Harvey Oswald. After entering the Rambler, Oswald and his companion would only have had to drive six blocks west on Elm Street and they would have been on Beckley Avenue and a straight shot to Oswald's rooming house. The Warren Commission could not accept this even though it might have given Oswald time to kill Tippit for having two men involved would have made it a conspiracy!

As to Lee Harvey Oswald shooting J. D. Tippit, let us examine the evidence: Dallas Police Unit #221 (Summers-refer-police radio log) stated on the police radio that he had an "eye ball" witness to the shooting. The suspect was a white male about twenty-seven, five feet, eleven inches, black wavy hair, fair complexioned, (not Oswald) wearing an Eisenhower-type jacket of light color, dark trousers, and a white shirt, apparently armed with a .32 caliber, dark-finish automatic pistol which he had in his right hand. (The jacket strongly resembles that worn by the driver of the station wagon).

Dallas Police Unit #550 Car 2 was driven to the scene of the Tippit murder by Sgt. Gerald Hill. He was accompanied by Bud Owens, Dallas Police Department, and William F. Alexander, Assistant D.A. for Dallas. Unit #550 Car 2 reported over the police radio that the shells at the scene indicated that the suspect was armed with a 38 caliber automatic. 38 automatic shells and 38 revolver shells are distinctly different. (Oswald allegedly had a 38 revolver in his possession when arrested?)

After much confusion in the Oak Cliff area the Dallas Police were finally directed to the Texas Theater where the suspect was reported to be. Several squads arrived at the theater and quickly surrounded it. At the back door was none other than William F. Alexander, Assistant D.A., and several Dallas Police officers with guns drawn. While Dallas Police Officer McDonald and others entered the theater and turned on the lights and the suspect was pointed out to them, they started searching people several rows in front of Oswald, giving him a chance to run if he wanted to—right into the blazing guns of waiting officers!

This man had to be stopped. He was the most dangerous criminal in the history of the world. Here was a man who was able to go from one location to another with the swiftness of Superman, to change his physical characteristics at will and who pumped four automatic slugs into a police officer with a revolver—indeed a master criminal!

Well, back to the facts? Oswald was captured by Officer McDonald, who was out cold from one blow from the suspect and woke up to find he had arrested the suspect! (Nice going, Mac).

Later that afternoon I received word of the suspect's arrest and the fact that he was suspected of being involved in the President's death. I immediately thought of the man running down the grassy knoll. I made a telephone call to Capt. Will Fritz and gave him the description of the man I had seen and Fritz said, "that sounds like the suspect we have. Can you come up and take a look at him?"

I arrived at Capt. Fritz office shortly after 4:30 p.m. I was met by Agent Bookhout from the F.B.I., who took my name and place of employment. The door to Capt. Fritz' personal office was open and the blinds on the windows were closed, so that one had to look through the doorway in order to see into the room. I looked through the open door at the request of Capt. Fritz and identified the man who I saw running down the grassy knoll and enter the Rambler station wagon—and it WAS Lee Harvey Oswald.

Fritz and I entered his private office together. He told Oswald, "This man (pointing to me) saw you leave." At which time the suspect replied, "I told you people I did." Fritz, apparently trying to console Oswald, said, "Take it easy, son—we're just trying to find out what happened." Fritz then said, "What about the car?" Oswald replied, leaning forward on Fritz' desk, "That station wagon belongs to Mrs. Paine—don't try to drag her into this." Sitting back in his chair, Oswald said very disgustedly and very low, "Everybody will know who I am now."

At this time Capt. Fritz ushered me from his office, thanking me. I walked away saddened but relieved that it was the end of the day and I could go home, where I could try—at least for a little while—to put the tragedy and the day's events out of my mind. I was soon to find out that my troubles had only begun—for I had seen and heard too much that fateful day.

Saturday, November 23, 1963, I spent the day at home talking to my wife, Molly, about Friday's events and playing with Deanna and Terry, not knowing that the very next day would bring another tragic event which would affect not only my job but my entire future.

Like many other Americans, I was watching television on Sunday morning, November 24, 1963 when Jack Ruby shot Lee Harvey Oswald. I would like to clear up one thing at this point concerning Ruby's access to the basement of the city jail. The Warren Commission concluded that Dallas Police Officer R. E. Vaughn, through negligence, let Jack Ruby into the basement.

What they did not say is that Officer Vaughn was questioned extensively after the shooting and even submitted to a polygraph test, which he passed, showing that he did not let Jack Ruby go down the Main Street Ramp of the city jail. I have known Officer Vaughn for many years and feel that he is honest, conscientious and one of the finest people I have ever known. I feel that he was unjustly accused. However, bombing Vaughn was the easiest way out for Earl Warren's Commission.

CHAPTER 3

The industrial and military complex can't survive

Without their little horror wars they artfully contrive

If they push us to the big one then we won't come out alive

His dream goes marching on

Things were fairly normal for me for the next few months, with the exception of curious persons who popped into the Sheriff's Office from time to time to ask me questions about the assassination.

On the first anniversary of the assassination a team of newsmen from NBC New York came to Dallas. They wanted to do a documentary on the assassination and they contacted Jim Kerr of the Dallas Times Herald who told them of me.

Jim approached me and said that the NBC people were interested in what I had to say and would I talk to them? Jim Kerr indicated to me that he had it all set up. However, because I knew how Bill Decker felt about anyone in his Department talking about this particular event, I told him I would have to get Decker's permission. NBC had been calling me since October 1964 asking to talk to me but I would not commit myself.

When they arrived during the week of November 22, I went to Decker to ask permission to do the story. Decker promptly sat me down in the private office, closed the door and sat there looking at me for several minutes. It was difficult to tell if Decker was looking at you—with that glass eye of his—but at the same time you had the uneasy feeling that he was looking straight through you. Decker began to talk with that even, never-rising voice which commanded attention and gave you the feeling that it was dangerous to interrupt or even question him.

Decker told me to tell these people (Jim Kerr and NBC) that I was a Deputy Sheriff—not an actor—and for me to keep my mouth shut. He then went on to say, "Tell them you didn't see or hear anything." He then went back to the papers on his desk and I knew he was through— and so was I. I relayed the message to Jim Kerr, who was very disappointed—and even mad, but he, like me, knew that he must not challenge Decker's law.

From that day forward Bill Decker began to watch my every move. People in the office who, before this, very seldom spoke to me, began to hang around watching my every move and listening to everything I said. Among these were Rosemary Allen, E. R. (Buddy) Walthers, Allen Sweatt and Bob Morgan—Decker's four top stoolies.

Combine the foregoing with the run-in I had with Dave Belin, junior counsel for the Warren Commission, who questioned me in April of 1964, and who changed my testimony fourteen times when he sent it to Washington, and you will have some idea of the pressures brought to bear.

David Belin told me who he was as I entered the interrogation room (April 1964). He had me sit at the head of a long table. To my left was a female with a pencil and pen. Belin sat to my right. Between the girl and Belin was a tape recorder, which was turned off. Belin instructed the girl not to take notes until he (Belin) said to do so. He then told me that the investigation was being conducted to determine the truth as the evidence indicates. Well, I could take that several ways but I said nothing. Then Belin said, "For instance, I will ask you where you were at a certain time. This will establish your physical location." It was at this point that I began to feel that I was being led into something but still I said nothing. Then Belin said, "I will ask you about what you thought you heard or saw in regard." Well, this was too much. I interrupted him and said, "Counselor, just ask me the questions and if I can answer them, I will." This seemed to irritate Belin and he told the girl to start taking notes with the next question.

At this point Belin turned the recorder on. The first questions were typical. Where were you born? Where did you go to school? When Belin would get to certain questions, he would turn off the recorder and stop the girl from writing. The he would ask me, for example, "Did you see anything unusual when you were behind the picket fence?" I said, "Yes" and he said, "Fine, just a minute." He would then tell the girl to start writing with the next question and would again start the recorder. What was the next question? "Mr. Craig, did you go into the Texas School Book Depository?" It was clear to me that he wanted only to record part of the interrogation, as this happened many times.

I finally managed to get in at least most of what I had seen and heard by ignoring his advanced questions and giving a step-by-step picture, which further seemed to irritate him.

At the end of our session Belin dismissed me but when I started to leave the room, he called me back. At this time, I identified the clothing worn by the suspect (the 26 volumes refer to a box of clothing—not boxes. There were two boxes.)

After I identified the clothing, Belin went over the complete testimony again. He then asked, "Do you want to follow or waive your signature or sign now?" Since there was nothing but a tape recording and a stenographer's note book, there was obviously nothing to sign. All other testimony which I have read (a considerable amount) included an explanation that the person could waive his signature then or his statement would be typed and he would be notified when it was ready for signature. Belin did not say this to me.

He said an odd thing when I left. It is the only time that he said it, and I have never read anything similar in any testimony. "Be SURE, when you get back to the office, to thank Sheriff Decker for his cooperation." I know of no one else he questioned who he asked to thank a supervisor, chief, etc.

I first saw my testimony in January of 1968 when I looked at the 26 volumes which belonged to Penn Jones. My alleged statement was included. The following are some of the changes in my testimony:

- Arnold Rowland told me that he saw two men on the sixth floor of the Texas School Book Depository 15 minutes before the President arrived: one was a Negro, who was pacing back and forth by the southwest window. The other was a white man in the southeast corner, with a rifle equipped with a scope, and that a few minutes later he looked back and only the white man was there. In the Warren Commission: Both were white, both were pacing in front of the southwest corner and when Rowland looked back, both were gone;
- I said the Rambler station wagon was light green. The Warren Commission: Changed to a white station wagon;
- I said the driver of the Station Wagon had on a tan jacket. The Warren Commission: A white jacket;
- I said the license plates on the Rambler were not the same color as Texas plates. The Warren Commission: Omitted the not—omitted but one word, an important one, so that it appeared that the license plates were the same color as Texas plates;
- I said that I got a good look at the driver of the Rambler. The Warren Commission: I did not get a good look at the Rambler. (In Captain Fritz's office) I had said that Fritz had said to Oswald, "This man saw you leave" (indicating me). Oswald said, "I told you people I did." Fritz then said, "Now take it easy, son, we're just trying to find out what happened", and then (to Oswald), "What about the car?" to which Oswald replied, "That

station wagon belongs to Mrs. Paine. Don't try to drag her into this." Fritz said car—station wagon was not mentioned by anyone but Oswald. (I had told Fritz over the telephone that I saw a man get into a station wagon, before I went to the Dallas Police Department and I had also described the man. This is when Fritz asked me to come there.) Oswald then said, "Everybody will know who I am now;" the Warren Commission: Stated that the last statement by Oswald was made in a dramatic tone. This was not so. The Warren Commission also printed, "NOW everybody will know who I am", transposing the now. Oswald's tone and attitude was one of disappointment. If someone were attempting to conceal his identity as Deputy and he was found out, exposed—his cover blown, his reaction would be dismay and disappointment. This was Oswald's tone and attitude—disappointment at being exposed!

Shortly after the Kerr and Belin incidents, the Sheriff took me out of the field and assigned me to the Bond Desk. This meant that I was sitting directly in line with Decker's office door, where he could watch me. It made me feel a little like a goldfish in a bowl!

While I was on the Bond Desk, I noticed Eva Grant (Jack Ruby's sister) was making daily visits to Decker's office. During this time Eva and I came to be on good terms. It was convenient for her to speak to me when she came in because of the position of my desk—close to the door leading into the Sheriff's Department. As time went on Eva Grant would stop me in the hall every time I went for a cup of coffee or took a break. Decker became very concerned over this and it was not long before I realized that ever time Eva and I talked we were joined by someone. In addition to this, Buddy Walthers would be standing close by and listening. (This is another example of his talents as a peace officer—that he would make himself so conspicuous.) First, he would stand and listen, and then head into Decker's office.

After a few days of this and armed with information from this so- called detective—who couldn't track an elephant through the snow with a nose bleed—Decker called me into his office and pointed to a chair without saying a word. Well, knowing he wasn't giving me the chair or asking me to look it over, I sat down. After a long silence he finally said, "What about it?" This was Decker's way of telling you he knew it (whatever it was) and he wanted you to "confess." I felt sure Eva Grant was going to be the subject of conversation but I was determined to make him start the interrogation—after all he wanted the answers and, apparently, Buddy had not heard as much as he thought he had.

Finally, he gave in and said, "You've been talking to Eva Grant." I said, "Yes sir." Decker then said, "What about?" I replied, "She is concerned about Jack's depressed state of mind and worried about the fact that he looks ill." Decker said, "That's none of your business." I replied with the only thing that Decker would accept—I said, "No sir." Apparently sure that he had convinced me once again that there was no law except Decker's law, he pointed to the door and I left. He was a man of few words!

The next day Eva and I had another talk. She was getting more and more concerned about Jack's health. She had been to see Decker several times trying to secure medical help for her brother. By this time the rumor was all through the Sheriff's office that Jack was, indeed, ill. Most of this information came from the deputies assigned to guard him. The deputies were Walter Neighbors, James R. Keene, Jess Stevenson, Jr., and others. Finally, Decker permitted a doctor to see Jack, a psychiatrist, who said Jack Ruby had a cold!

A few weeks passed, during which time I received some telephone calls concerning the assassination and my testimony. These calls came from various people from different parts of the country who were, apparently, just interested. These calls somehow were reported to Bill Decker. Not having a reason to fire me, he did the next best thing, he had a monitoring unit connected to the telephone system so that he could periodically check any telephone calls.

I will not go into the events leading to Jack Ruby's death. Much has already been written about this but I would like to say that Jack Ruby made several statements to guards, jail supervisors and assistant D.A.'s in which he said "they are going to kill me." These statements became a private joke among these people and they discussed them freely in the hall of the court house. When the Sheriff from Wichita Falls, Texas came to observe the prisoner he was about to take charge of, due to Ruby's change of venue, he refused to accept the prisoner on the grounds that Ruby was very ill. Then, and only then, did Decker send Ruby to Parkland Hospital where he died a few short days later (some cold!).

I was not too concerned about the minor attention I was receiving from Decker regarding the assassination and its aftermath until August 7, 1966. At 2:30 a.m, I was approached by Hardy M. Parkerson, an attorney from New Orleans, La. Mr. Parkerson was interested in the assassination and the Jack Ruby trial. I was working late nights on the Bond Desk when he came to the Sheriff's office. He asked me several questions relating to these tragic events and I answered him as honestly as I could and he thanked me and left.

However, on October 1, 1966 Mr. Parkerson wrote to me advising me that I was receiving more publicity than I might be aware of. He mentioned in his letter that he had picked up a book on a New Orleans newsstand. The book was entitled, The Second Oswald by Richard H. Popkin and my report had been mentioned in the book. This disturbed me as I knew my popularity with Decker was fading anyway.

On October 18 I received another letter from Mr. Parkerson. It seemed that he had come across another book on a New Orleans newsstand which mentioned my name. This one was Inquest by Edward J. Epstein. Then I began to worry a bit. Of course, other names were mentioned also in these books, but I was concerned because of my employer's attitude and the fact that I was in definite conflict with the Warren Commission in my testimony.

In February of 1967 the lid blew off. District Attorney Jim Garrison announced publicly his probe into the John F. Kennedy Assassination. It wasn't long—in fact, a matter of hours — until Decker walked up to me and asked,

"Have you been talking to Jim Garrison?" I told him that I had not, which was the truth. Decker then said, "Somebody sure as hell has." That was the beginning of the end of my career as a law officer and my future in Dallas County.

As more and more books critical of the Warren Commission began to hit the newsstands throughout the country and I received calls and visitors asking questions my future with the Sheriff's Office became very shaky. Finally, on July 4, 1967 Bill Decker called me into his office and told me to check out. Knowing there was no grievance board and that Decker was the supreme ruler of his domain, I left the Sheriff's Office for good.

I was saddened by the loss of eight years in a job that I had given my ALL to. But I was soon to find out that this was only the down payment on the price that I was to pay for the truth! I immediately began looking for work and found that the Commerce Bail Bond Company was just opening an office and needed someone to help in the office as Les Hancock, the owner, was just starting out.

Mr. Hancock and I had a long talk and he agreed that I would be an asset to the business because he knew nothing about it and I was familiar with bonds and most of the people at the Sheriff's Office as well as those wishing to make bond. Les and I seemed to get along very well. I posted most of the bonds and kept track of our clients. Posting the first few bonds with the county went slowly—although the money was in escrow, Decker wanted to personally approve all bonds posted by me. I did not mind this delaying tactic because all it involved was a little extra time for me. The bonding business was going very well—within two months we were making money.

I kept up as much as possible on Jim Garrison's probe and decided to write him and tell him what I knew—if it would help him. Jim Garrison answered my letter and asked me to call him, at which time he made arrangements for my trip to New Orleans.

Les Hancock tried to persuade me not to go, saying I shouldn't get involved (a little late). I arrived in New Orleans in late October and was picked up at the airport by Bill Boxley, one of Jim's investigators, and four men who didn't work for Jim. Boxley took me to a motel where I was to meet Jim and the other four men followed—apparently, they were not invited. Most of my talks with Jim were at his office while my "tails" (apparently government agents) searched my room. I must apologize to them for not bringing what they could "use."

I had several meetings with Jim Garrison. He showed me numerous pictures taken in Dealey Plaza on November 22, 1963. Among them was a picture of a Latin male. I recognized him as being the same man I had seen driving the Rambler station wagon in which I had seen Oswald leave the Book Depository area. I was surprised and I asked Jim who the man was. Jim did not know but he did say this man was arrested in Dealey Plaza immediately after the assassination but was released by Dallas Police because he could not speak English! This was, to me, highly unusual. In my experience as a police officer I had never known of a person (or prisoner) being released because of a language barrier. Interpreters were, of course, always available.

We also discussed the 45 caliber slug found on the south side of Elm Street, in the grass, by E. R. (Buddy) Walthers. Buddy had indeed found such a slug. He and I discussed it the evening of November 22, 1963. Buddy also gave a statement to the Dallas Press confirming this find (found among bits of brain matter). However, he later denied finding it—after Decker had a long talk with him and subsequent to newsmen questioning the Sheriff about the evidence.

Jim Garrison also had a picture of an unidentified man picking up this 45 slug and Buddy is also in that photograph. I asked Buddy about this many times—after his denial—but he never made any comment.

Jim also asked me about the arrests made in Dealey Plaza that day. I told him I knew of twelve arrests, one in particular made by R. E. Vaughn of the Dallas Police Department. The man Vaughn arrested was coming from the Dal-Tex Building across from the Texas School Book Depository. The only thing which Vaughn knew about him was that he was an independent oil operator from Houston, Texas. The prisoner was taken from Vaughn by Dallas Police detectives and that was the last that he saw or heard of the suspect.

Incidentally, there are no records of any arrests, either by the Dallas Police Department or the Sheriff's Office, made in Dealey Plaza on November 22, 1963. Very strange! Any and all arrests made during my eight years as an officer were recorded. It may not have been entered as a record with the Identification Bureau but a report was always typed and a permanent record kept—if only in our case files. A report on any questioning shows a reason for your action and protects you against false arrest. I am saying that there is absolutely no record in the case files or any place else.

Upon returning to Dallas from my first contact with Jim Garrison, I was picked up by another "tail." I was followed constantly after that. My wife could not even go to the grocery store without being followed. Sometimes they would go so far as to pull up next to her and make sure she saw them talking on their two-way radios. They would also park across from my house and sit for hours making sure I knew they were there.

On the morning of November 1, 1967, I received a call from a friend of mine. He owned a night club at Carroll and Columbia Streets in Dallas. Bill said that he wanted to see me and would I meet him in front of the club. Bill had called me many times when I was a deputy as he was frequently in financial trouble and I would have the citation issued for him held up until he was in a position to accept them. Some people in Dallas did receive Special Treatment in the matter of citations. Bill was not one of these but I did this for him because I knew that by holding it up a day or so I could save his credit rating—and the creditor would be paid without having a Judgment entered. We were friends and it was a natural—and practical thing to do.

When Bill called me on November 1st, he said he wanted to talk to me about money he owed the Bonding Company where I worked—for getting one of his employees out of jail on traffic tickets. He had asked that I meet him at 9:00 a.m. At about 8:30 a.m. "me and my shadows" started for the club, arriving at approximately 9:00 a.m.

When I parked in front of Bill's club "my shadows" began one of the sweetest set-ups I had ever seen. One car, a tan Pontiac, parked one block in front of my car, racing me, and the other, a white Chevrolet with a small antenna protruding from the roof, kept circling the block again and again, never stopping. There were two men in the Chevrolet. I couldn't get a good look at the driver but the other man was in his early thirties. He had dark hair, was nice looking and wore a black-and-white checked sport coat.

Bill had never been late before for an appointment with me but he was this time. When it was nearing 10:15 I began to worry that those poor bastards would get dizzy from driving around and around—and might hit someone.

Finally, at 10:15 a.m. Bill arrived and we went to the Waffle House across the street for coffee. There, as big as life, sitting on a stool was the man in the sport jacket—from the white Chevrolet. Well . . . we sat down and had coffee. We talked about how each of us was doing—just shot the bull—and Bill never did bring up the subject which he had said he wanted to discuss with me!

When we finished, we started to leave and the man in the sport coat jumped up and beat us out of the door. We paid our checks and walked out the door and my shadow was nowhere in sight—believe me, I looked. We crossed the parking lot and stopped at the traffic light, as it was red against us. For some reason I stepped down off the curb before the light changed. As I did, Bill fell flat on the sidewalk. I was about to find out why. At that very instant a shot rang out behind me and the hair just above my left ear parted. I felt a pressure and sharp pain on the left side of my head. I bolted for my car leaving Bill lying on the ground. I heard him say, "You son of a bitch" and I jumped into my car and drove home as fast as possible. When I arrived home, I told my wife what this good friend had done for me. I pondered the idea of moving my family to some safe place.

A curious note: my friend (?) Bill was deeply in debt and about to lose his business at the time of the shooting. However, about a month later he was completely out of debt, his business was doing great and he had invested in two other businesses which were doing very well. (Payment was, apparently, not withheld just because the trigger man missed.) I decided to get in touch with Jim Garrison. I tried all day and finally reached him around ten that evening. After I told him what had happened, he said someone would be at my home within the hour.

At approximately 11 p.m. someone knocked on the door and I opened it with my left hand, holding my 45 automatic in my right hand. Standing there was a small but well-built man in his late forties or early fifties. He said, "My name is Penn Jones. Jim Garrison called me." My hand tightened on the 45 when my wife, Molly, took hold of me and said, "I've seen him on T.V. He is Penn Jones." With that I relaxed and he remained Penn Jones!

Penn Jones listened to my story and then began making telephone calls to newsmen and wire services that he had contact with, explaining to me that the best protection for me was open coverage on the incident. After a long talk with Penn Jones I found that I had a great deal of respect and admiration for this man. Although small in stature, I felt he would fight the devil himself to find the truth about the assassination.

The next day, November 2, 1967, when I went to work at Commerce Bail Bonds, I was approached by two reporters and a photographer from Channel 8 in Dallas. They had picked the story up on the news wire and wanted a personal interview. After the interview my boss, Les Hancock, called me into his office and told me he didn't think that I should have done the interview (giving no specific reason).

The next few days Les' attitude was very cold and he would barely speak to me. Then, on the 7th of November he called me into his office once again. This time he told me the business wasn't doing well and he would have to let me go because he was closing the office. Of course, I knew better than this—after all I had access to all the records and I knew the business was making money. A few days later I found out Les merely moved to another location and his business continued as usual.

However, this knowledge did not help me for I was back pounding the pavement looking for work. In the meantime, I had been in contact with Jim Garrison. He informed me that there was an opening at Volkswagen International in New Orleans and that I might try there. By this time my health had begun to be affected. I had undergone a serious stomach operation in August of 1963 and I suffer from chronic bronchitis and emphysema (not to mention Dallas County Battle Fatigue).

My family and I made the trip to New Orleans, where I was interviewed by Willard Robertson, the owner of the company. Mr. Robertson told me he was looking for a Personnel Manager and because of my background of dealing with the public he hired me. After a long trip back to Dallas where we gathered up our meager belongings we moved to New Orleans and I felt good—I was working again!

We had been there but a few days when all of our neighbors and half the people where I was working knew who I was. This was due to the newspaper and television coverage of Jim Garrison's probe into the assassination. Again came the never-ending questions, which I did not mind because outside of Dallas people were sincerely interested and I certainly did not mind doing what I could to clear up any doubts they had. The people at the office treated me very well.

Unfortunately, after about a month I realized that I was not doing anything but going in to the office and coming home—nothing in between. Although I appreciated Jim Garrison recommending me for the job, I knew by this time that he had done this because he was concerned about my safety and wanted me out of Dallas. Because this company did not really need a Personnel Manager and I couldn't take the money for a job I was not doing, I submitted my resignation to Mr. Robertson and my family and I returned to Dallas.

We arrived back in Dallas on a cold and snowy seventh of January, 1968, and moved in with Molly's parents as we had very little money and nowhere to stay. The next few days I spent looking for work. I tried every ad and every lead I could find. The people who interviewed me always seemed interested but like all companies, they wanted to check out my references. When I failed to receive any results from my efforts, I called some of the places where I had placed applications to see what was wrong. I always received the same answer, "the position had been filled." Finally, I decided something was wrong and I suspected one employment reference, Bill Decker. I had a friend write Decker asking for an employment reference—he never received an answer!

My next move was to have someone call Decker and ask for a reference and this took some doing. Writing him was one thing but talking to him on the telephone was another. He would bait you on the telephone and, before you knew it, he knew who you were and whether you were legitimate or not.

Many people in Dallas liked Decker for the favors he could do for them but those who did not like him were afraid of the tremendous power he possessed in Dallas County. They were afraid to oppose him in any issue for fear that this man could, indeed, affect their professional careers. A good example is the charge, "Hold for Decker." This meant that when Decker wanted to talk to you or some friend of his disagreed with an arrest (without warrant), you were detained in the county jail until Decker wished to talk or release you. No attorney in Dallas County would dare apply for a writ of habeas corpus to secure your release.

Well, to get back to my "minor" problem, I finally found someone to call Decker for a reference and when he did Decker informed him that, "Mr. Craig had worked for me and I would not re-hire him and that is all I've got to say about Mr. Craig." So . . . I had worked for the Sheriff for eight years and yet, without a reference, it was as though those years had never existed. How do you explain this kind of situation to a prospective employer?

After many more exhaustive interviews, I found a company, on February 1, 1968, which had just opened a branch office in Dallas and was in BAD need of security guards to work in department stores where they had new contracts. When I applied for the job I told them of my background in law enforcement, leaving out the details of my separation with the Sheriff's Office. I only showed them the watch I was wearing, which is inscribed: Roger D. Craig, First Place, Sheriff's Department 1960. (The award was for Officer of the Year). They were impressed and with a sigh of relief I was hired without the customary background check.

My first assignment was a department store in East Dallas, where I held the very important position of keeping the shopping baskets out of the aisles. (Don't knock it—I was working 12 hours a day and making a whopping $1.60 per hour).

By this time my creditors were knocking on my door day and night. All of the furniture we had, which was not much, we lost and then "along came Jones."

I had contacted Penn when I arrived back in Dallas and after I lost the car he let me use his 1955 Ford, which he wasn't driving, and I was back in business!

Because of the crowded quarters at Molly's parents, we began to search for an apartment. We found many and were turned down every time. Some people said they did not want to rent to families with children. Others would accept us and then when we were ready to move in, they would say it was already rented and they had "forgotten." Finally, in mid- February we found a couple on Tremont Street, who were not afraid to rent to us. Oh, they knew who I was but they said it did not matter— they had kept up on the assassination.

Our only outlet for our tensions were the Sunday trips we made to the Penn Jones home in Midlothian, Texas. During these visits I would try to bring Penn up to date on the latest from the Dallas Police Department and Sheriff's Office. I was able to give him some help from time to time because I could keep in touch with these offices through officers there who were still friendly toward me. It was fun and relaxing to get together with Penn and his wife L.A., who is a delightful person with a great sense of humor. The two of them made you feel as though the whole world was right there.

On one of these visits Penn told me he was going to appear on the Joe Pyne show in Los Angeles and asked if I would go with him. Needless to say, I owed Penn Jones much over the previous months and if I would be an asset, I was certainly prepared to go, I told him. I got a leave of absence from my employer, Penn made the arrangements and we were off to Los Angeles.

The Los Angeles trip was a success as far as I was concerned, especially when we spoke to the young people at U.C.L.A. They were very concerned about the assassination and were kind to Penn and me. The only disappointment came in the form of Otto Preminger, who was sitting in for Joe Pyne that night. I think his statement to the audience speaks for itself. He said that he believed whole-heartedly in the Warren Report and when I asked him if he had read the Warren Report, he said "no"! After a week of appearances on television and radio my lungs were beginning to give me trouble and I returned to Dallas with Mrs. Jones, while Penn went on to San Francisco.

After a few weeks back on my important job of keeping the shopping carts in line I found that at a dollar and sixty cents an hour I had too much month left at the end of the money. We were behind on our rent and, oh well, back to the want ads.

We found a couple who were looking for someone to live in and care for their elderly mother, rent free. After all this time there was something free? Getting settled did not take very long—with just a few clothes. This worked out fairly well. I worked twelve hours a day and Molly did all of the washing, ironing, cooking and cleaning—in addition to caring for Terry, Deanna and Roger Jr. (Who had been staying previously with his grandmother). Did I say free?

In the meantime, Penn had returned from San Francisco and during a visit to our house he told me he could get me a job in Midlothian working at an oil refinery and that the pay was $500.00 per month. I hated to give up the prestige of my present position but money was money. I gave my employer notice and on April 15, 1968 I started work at the refinery. This was not crude oil but used motor oil—we re-re- processed it. The work was new to me and I had never re-refined used motor oil before. I found that I was a little soft. I had to dump three thousand pounds (50 fifty-pound bags) of clay into hot oil every morning and pump it back into the still which cooked it. This whipped me into shape quite rapidly. I was not concerned with the physical work involved for I knew that I had a chance to support my family and that was what counted.

The work went smoothly until the second Thursday of May, 1968 when, while trying to start an engine at the plant, I slipped and broke my arm— "good ole lady luck." I had my arm set and missed one day of work. On Monday morning I returned to work, knowing I could not live on workmen's compensation, which was about $40.00 per week. I painfully continued to work with the arm in a cast for the next six weeks.

During this six-week period my boss had offered to let me move into a house he owned in Midlothian so that I would be closer to work. I took him up on the offer because I was driving sixty miles each day to work and back and Molly was worried about me driving and working with the broken arm and—again I was being followed.

During this time a Dallas Sheriff's car stopped me and asked where I was going. I had known this deputy for several years and there was no reason for his behavior. Molly's health was getting worse. She had serious stomach disorders and the strain of past events had not helped— so we moved. Now we were in Midlothian and I was driving four miles to work and back.

During the time I was still driving back and forth from Dallas to Midlothian—or the job—I noticed that I was being followed by a blue and white pick-up, occupied by a white male. One day, after being followed by this truck for several days, as the truck was approaching the driver stuck a revolver out the window and was about to fire, when another car pulled up behind me and he withdrew the pistol. My hours were never the same two days in a row but this man seemed to know the precise hour I would leave work. Penn Jones and I tried to set a trap for this man but, he, apparently knew it and got away. I never saw him after that.

It was six weeks since I had broken my arm and this was the day I was to have the cast taken off. I felt good as it had been quite a burden. On that morning I reported for work and started preparing the pumps and tanks for cooking the oil when lady luck smiled down on me once again. I started to light the furnace and it blew up, burning my face and a good deal of hair and my arms. This was around the first of July, 1968. After the doctor treated me, he advised me that I would have to wear the cast another two weeks because he was afraid that I would get an infection in the burned area if the cast were removed. I do not want to leave the impression that my conflict with the Dallas establishment was the direct cause of these accidents. However, had the door not been closed to me in Dallas, I would not have had to turn to work with which I was not familiar.

In August of 1968 (while living in Midlothian) I received a visit in the middle of the night from a man in his fifties who said he was out of gas. I was already in bed and Molly was catching up on some of my court records when this man came to the door. Molly told him I was in bed with a sprained ankle and would not be able to help him. She directed him to the neighbors down the road. He went straight to his car, which was parked beside our house, got in, started it right up and drove off! Apparently, he was not out of gas but wanted us to know we could be found. This was about the time Penn was printing some pretty hot editorials in his paper with information I had supplied. I guess someone didn't like it.

I made some friends in Midlothian and was getting along fairly well. I had a job, a place to live and was able to purchase a used car.

The City Council was taking applications for a city judge. After talking it over with Penn Jones and some of my other friends, I went before the council for an interview, and, I must say, it was somewhat of a surprise when they appointed me. The future was beginning to show some promise. I continued the work at the refinery and pursued my new duties at city hall.

On August 5, 1968, Bill Seward, the only other employee at the refinery, was discussing a better way to process the oil with Dale Foshee, the owner. They were going to try something new in an attempt to obtain a better quality of oil. Dale purchased a new type of clay which would absorb more waste from the used oil as it cooked. Neither of these men told me that this new clay contained a substantial amount of some sort of acid. This meant that when I dumped it (the clay) into the hot oil tank, as I did every morning, and did not wear any sort of breathing devise, I inhaled a great deal of the dust from this new product.

Shortly after I started cooking the oil, I noticed I was having trouble breathing. I did not pay much attention to it and finished the day's work. That night the acid really got to me and I found myself passing out. I tried lying my head right in the window to get enough air—but still could not. Penn Jones came to the house and he and Molly rushed me to the hospital in Mansfield, Texas, about ten miles from Midlothian. I stayed under an oxygen tent for two days. On the fourth day I felt much better and was released from the hospital.

I had learned, about a week before going to the hospital, that the Justice of the Peace in Midlothian was resigning and I was persuaded by friends to seek that position. I had talked with the county commissioners before I went to the hospital and they made their final decision on the day I came home from the hospital. I was sworn in as Justice of the Peace on August 8, 1968. I would be an appointee until the November election. Now I was working at the refinery, holding the position of City Judge and also Justice of the Peace. The city paid me $50.00 a month and the Justice of the Peace position brought in about $50.00 a month. I was not getting rich but look at it this way, I was the entire establishment in Midlothian!

The business for the city was very routine and went rather smoothly. However, the Justice Court was another matter. I was having to correspond with the surrounding counties and they were all cooperative, with one exception (you guessed it), Dallas County. Some warrants, citations and subpoenas were sent to the Dallas County Sheriff for service. Needless to say, they were returned "unable to locate"!

So, the door was still closed to me in Dallas — even in matters of the law which these officials were sworn to uphold. Now, also Decker knew where I was and it was not long before my creditors, with whom I had been trying to make arrangements to pay a little to each month, had obtained judgments against me in the Dallas courts and I had been served with the papers. Now there was no hope of clearing my credit without paying everyone in full, which was impossible (I'll bet his glass was really shining). The next few weeks I managed to avoid my contact with the Good People of Dallas, hoping that they would forget about me—a fat chance!

In October 1968, my oldest son (Roger, Jr.) wasn't doing well in school and he decided to run away from home. I was, of course, very concerned about him—he was only fourteen years old. I contacted the Dallas Morning News to see if they would print his picture. I might have just as well invaded Russia. My name was immediately connected with Jim Garrison and before I could say stop the press, my name and connection with Jim was all over the newspaper, UPI, radio and television. I was getting calls from all over the country.

A couple of days later we received a call from the sheriff in Texarkana, Arkansas. He had Roger Jr. We went to Arkansas and retrieved him as quietly as possible. He had been working for one day on a ranch.

On October the seventh I reported to work at the refinery at which time my boss handed me a check marked, FINAL. He told me he was cutting down on production due to a slowdown in business and he wouldn't need me anymore. Now where have I heard that before?

Being Justice of the Peace, I wasn't without influence in Midlothian. I soon secured a job at a gas station changing truck tires. Not much prestige but a lot of hours and I quickly commanded the respect of every tire tool in the place.

A few days later, my former employer came to me and said that I would have to move out of his house because he wanted to use if for a week retreat to get away from Dallas.

By this time I was beginning to suspect the periodic publicity I had been receiving through the years, might have had something to do with my trouble finding jobs and housing. I guess I am a little slow—especially when this former employer hired someone to take my place at the refinery. He let him move into the house where I lived—as I found out sometime later. So now I had to work 12 hours a day and try to find a place to move my family. The election was coming up. This would not have been important except for the fact that being Justice of the Peace served as a deterrent from harassment by certain people, whose names I need not mention.

It was November and I still had been unable to find a house to rent. Midlothian was a very small town and there were just no houses to rent.

Anyway, the election was over and I had won by twenty votes. No doubt, twenty people who did not read the paper or watch television. I continued working at the gas station and living in my former employer's house. The election had done at least one thing for me. Dale still wanted me to move but was not pressing as hard. The days which followed were hard—we had rain and some sleet and working in this was beginning to affect my health. Molly was ill and Deanna, who had suffered from chronic bronchitis since birth, was not doing any better than we were. December was on us before I knew it and Mr. Roberts, the owner, decided to retire from the gas station. This meant, of course, that I was back on the street.

CHAPTER 4

Our President is lying up there cold beneath his flame

He is calling out for vengeance and to do so in his

name To keep the peace forever and erase our nation's

shame His dream goes marching on

This time there were no jobs to be found. However, business in the Justice Court was somewhat improved due to the opening of a substation in Midlothian by the Highway Patrol. I could not pay the rent or meet the bills but the increase was enough to buy groceries. I had resigned as City Judge so that there would be no conflict of interest between the two positions (City and County Court).

It was at this time that I was notified by District Attorney, Jim Garrison, that he would need me in the upcoming Clay Shaw trial—another wrench in the machinery. The night after I was notified of this, I received a telephone call and the voice asked if I was going to go to New Orleans. When I answered, "yes," he just said, "get a one-way ticket" and then hung up. I brushed this off as just another crank. I'd had those calls before. However, the next day I received another call. This time it was a different voice. This one asked if I were going to New

Orleans and when I said, "yes," all he said was, "Remember you have a family" and hung up.

I must admit this worried me. After that I would get up during the night and check the family and house—not a very pleasant way to live.

During this turmoil I at last had a prospect of getting back into that illusive pastime called "employment"—it was again Penn Jones to the rescue—and I say this with the greatest respect and admiration! Penn had been corresponding with a friend of his in Boulder, Colorado, regarding helping me find employment out of Texas, which seemed the only thing left. The friend suggested to Penn that I make a trip to Boulder to check into some leads so the Jones family made the arrangements and I was off to Boulder. This was in January 1969.

I arrived in Boulder and was met by members of the Students for a Democratic Society, whose names I will not mention. (J. Edgar Hoover should not have his work made so easy). They took me from the airport and arranged for my lodging. The next three days I filled out applications at various places, including the Boulder Police Department and Sheriff's Office because those were the positions I was most qualified for and I believed I could be a cop and still have compassion for my fellow men. If they would not accept me that way, I could always quit—after all, I was an expert at being out of work.

After I had exhausted all possibilities, I thanked the people who had been so kind to me and returned to Midlothian, Texas to wait. I had been home about one week when I received word from the Boulder Sheriff's Department that there would be an opening soon and if I wanted the job, it was mine. Satisfied that the out of Texas bit was going to pay off, the Penn Jones, bless them, financed the trip back to Boulder. This time the family went with me. We drove straight through from Midlothian to Boulder. The second day in Boulder we found an apartment or two we might be able to afford until I started getting regular pay checks. I felt good about having a chance at a new start as I went to see Under Sheriff Cunningham.

When I arrived at the Sheriff's Department, Cunningham took me to his office, asked me to sit down and closed the door. It was then that I began to get that feeling I'd had so many times before when I was about to get the purple shaft. Sure enough, I had managed to lose a job before I even started. Mr. Cunningham began to ask me about my background with the Dallas Sheriff's Department (which he already knew from my previous visit) and the reason for my termination. Then he brought out his big gun, "What about Jim Garrison?" Well, knowing I'd been had, I told him I was going to have to testify in the Shaw trial (which I'm sure he already knew).

I'd heard about every excuse there was for not hiring me but he should have handed me this one in a gift-wrapped "surprise" package. "Mr. Craig," he said, (I had been Roger until then) "we've had a little situation here" and he went on—it seemed that one of their jailers had seduced a sixteen-year-old girl while she was in their custody—WOW—and with that and my connection with the Garrison probe, the heat would be more than they wanted to handle. He was sorry. So was I—all the way back to Texas.

When we arrived back in Midlothian, we were all exhausted and very disappointed. Molly had the flu, Deanna a bad cold and the strain of the past few weeks had taken its toll on me. I was having trouble with my stomach and lungs and was down to 138 pounds. It was February 1, 1969. We had just enough money left from the trip to perhaps rent a house and buy a few groceries. Dale Foshee was pressing me again to move and I had nowhere to go and no prospects of a job. Like a wounded animal, I could only think of returning to familiar surroundings—the place that I had spent most of my adult life.

We drove to Dallas and by some streak of luck sneaked by a property owner and managed to rent a house. Before this poor, misguided soul could change his mind, we gathered up our belongings in Midlothian and moved back to Dallas, where I again applied my trade of looking for work.

I spent the following days filling out many applications and some of the interviews were even promising. I was very careful not to mention any part of my involvement in the assassination.

However, on February 13, 1969 I was summoned to New Orleans to testify in the Clay Shaw trial. On the 14th when I finally took the stand the defense tried very hard to discredit me by saying that I worked in New Orleans and was, in fact, still working in that city under an assumed name. Failing to discredit me, they accomplished the next best thing, the distorted version appeared in newspapers and wire services throughout the country.

WHEN THEY KILL A PRESIDENT

When I returned to Dallas on February 16, 1969, I was to realize the full impact of this distorted news story, for when I contacted the job possibilities I had before I testified, I found all doors closed. On March 4—after several days of no openings, or being told that I was not qualified, or that they would call me, which they never did—I found a job with Industrial Towel and Uniform Company of Dallas. This was a rental company and they needed men so that all I had to do was pass a polygraph test to prove I was not a thief, which I passed!

Now I was a Route Salesman. Ponder that awhile—a Judge reduced to picking up dirty laundry. Oh, well, work is work! Still weak and underweight from being sick during January and February, I was determined to make it on my new job.

I left home at 5:45 a.m. and arrived at the plant a little after 6:00 a.m., put my route slips in order, loaded my truck and started my deliveries. I got back to the plant about 4:30 p.m., unloaded the dirty linens, turned in my money and charge slips and got back home around 6:30 p.m. This was the season for cold, rainy weather—wouldn't you know? I had been to a doctor who gave me some medication for the chest infection I had developed and the medicine kept me going until March 14—when I, literally, ran out of gas.

On March 18, Molly called Penn and told him that I was not any better. Penn began to make arrangements for me to be admitted to the Veterans Hospital, where he was to meet me. By this time, I was out of it and Molly called an ambulance. I had completely passed out by the time it had arrived. I knew that I was going to the V.A. Hospital but when I woke up a short time later, I knew I was not at the

V.A. Hospital. Those dirty bastards had taken me to Parkland Hospital, which has a reputation for saving people comparable to my employment record for the past two years. I gathered what strength I had, got off the stretcher and staggered down the hall.

Molly had reached Penn, who was waiting at the V.A. Hospital, and he was madder than hell as he hated Parkland Hospital even more than I did. So, I finally wound up at the V.A. Hospital via Penn's car, where I spent the next ten days. I was released from the hospital on March 28, 1969 with instructions not to work out in the weather until my lungs had improved. This, of course, eliminated my job as a route salesman.

I knew an inside job was going to be hard to find from my experience during the past two years. First of all, I knew that when my references were checked Decker would not give me a favorable recommendation— if he even gave one at all. Second, my unstable employment record during the past two years had resulted in a disastrous credit rating. Eight years of experience in various responsible duties at the Sheriff's Office were gone. They had, indeed, done their work well!

After many weeks of search, I still had no job and was again behind on the rent. At this point we took two cameras, one 8 millimeter movie and one Minor still, our projector and screen and sold them for enough to rent a cheaper house. We moved into a three-room house on Gurley Street which wasn't much but it kept out the rain!

One day I got a wild idea. I would go down to the Federal Building and apply for a government job—those people will hire anybody—well, almost anybody. I passed the civil service test and was told they had a job coming up in the office and I was qualified for it. I was to go back in two days to begin work. Things were certainly looking up. I went over to my father-in-law's and drank all of his beer to celebrate.

The two days passed and I headed for my government job, which was to be handling correspondence from other government agencies—they do a lot of writing to each other. Well, when I arrived, I was ushered into one of those cubby hole offices AGAIN, where I was told that they had received a memo telling them the budget was being cut and my job was being eliminated (I hadn't even started). Oh, well, at least I was losing "more important" jobs now.

On June 1st I answered an ad for an Assistant Manager's job at a liquor store, where the only qualification was that I pass another polygraph test, which I did, proving that I had not yet turned to stealing. The next day I reported for work to find that I was a delivery boy again. My job was restocking private clubs throughout Dallas who bought merchandise from the store. I soon made friends with all the club owners, and every time I would make a delivery, they would insist on buying me a drink. I was making $1.87 an hour. I wasn't the highest paid delivery boy in town but after a few stops I was probably the happiest!

In the meantime, being out of work from March until June 1st, I was again behind on the rent as well as the car payment on my used 1965 Buick. The landlord had asked us to move. I tried to explain my situation and the fact that I was now working and would try to catch up on the rent but he didn't care—I had to go. It was two weeks before

I received a pay check. I don't know how we made it but we did. Molly then found a house for us to rent and I paid the first month's rent. I didn't worry about the car payment any longer for two days after I started to work the bank repossessed the car. We then again went back to driving one of Penn's cars.

During the slow periods of the weeks which followed I was always searching the paper and talking to people—trying to find a better paying job with a little security. I was working eleven hours a day, six days a week so it took me some time to locate one and I also had to be careful not to let people know too much about me because the general attitude in Dallas was not to get involved in the assassination. (A little late for Dallas).

On September 18, 1969 I applied at Peakload, Inc., a temporary employment service, who was looking for a dispatcher. The job consisted of taking orders from companies which needed temporary help for a few days, selecting the men from the hall who were best suited to the customer's needs, then seeing that they were delivered by our driver and picked up promptly after work. Al Nagel, the office manager, was from Minnesota and knew little of the events in Dallas and nothing of the people involved in the assassination so I slipped by and was hired. Now I was doing something which I enjoyed and the pay was $500.00 a month with time and one-half for over 48 hours. The next few weeks went by swiftly. I was working six days a week and making enough money to pay the rent, buy groceries and clothes for the kids.

On November 10, 1969 I was taken to the V.A. Hospital again. This time with neuritis, which the doctors said was caused by a vitamin deficiency over a long period of time, and bronchial pneumonia. This time I was not too concerned because Al Nagel liked my work and I was sure that I had a future with Peakload regardless of this temporary setback.

Well, after twenty-four days of what seemed like endless injections of vitamins, penicillin and streptomycin (one hundred and twenty-eight in all) I was sent home on December 4, 1969. The next day I called Al Nagel to tell him that I would return to work in a couple of days—when I got my strength back. Al informed me that I no longer had the job— that I had been replaced.

My final check from Peakload paid the rent for a month and bought a few groceries but Christmas was coming and I had managed somehow not to let the kids down—up until now. While I was in the hospital Penn Jones brought a letter he had received from Madeline Goddard. She had, apparently, read much on the assassination and sent her best wishes and support to us. Also, in the letter was the answer to this Christmas. Madeline had enclosed a check for $100.00.

She did not realize it, I'm sure, but that kept us from throwing my hands up in the air and giving up. The next few weeks were a repetition of earlier days—no jobs, no money, no prospects (there must be a song in there somewhere). Our only means of eating those days was Madeline Goddard's generosity; God bless Madeline and her generous heart.

Penn Jones had a few acres of land in Boyce, Texas, a short distance from Midlothian and he had persuaded us to move into the smaller of two houses on this land. We decided to go so that I could recuperate and regroup my thoughts. By this time, January 24, 1970, I was very depressed and ready to throw in the towel.

Penn and his son, Penn III, moved our belongings into the small three- room house and I must say that the fresh air and freedom from Dallas and its citizens was a welcome change. After a few days I felt better and began exploring our new surroundings. Penn had seventy-eight head of cattle on the place and I was feeding twenty bales of hay to them every morning. As my strength came back I also tackled various small, clean up jobs around the farm. It was the least I could do—the rent was free and Penn paid the light and water bills. We bought what butane we had to buy for heat and cooking. How about this—in 1948 I ran away from home at age 12 and spent the next four years working on farms and ranches in the west and northwest—now twenty-two years later I was back on the farm! There were days, however, when the rain and sleet would keep me inside, only venturing out when I had to (mostly to feed the cows).

The highlight of each day was when the mail man came as we were now corresponding with Madeline Goddard regularly and always looked forward to her letters. I do not know what we would have done if it hadn't been for this wonderful person. If I live to be a hundred, I couldn't repay her!

Roger Jr. was sixteen now and living with his grandparents in Dallas. Terry and Deanna were going to school in Waxahachie, seven miles away. They had to walk about three quarters of a mile to the school bus stop so in bad weather we would drive them to school. This was no easy job in the 1955 Ford of Penn's, which had seen better days. I certainly do not mean to sound ungrateful—Penn Jones and his wife were wonderful to us—we will always hold them close.

It was April when the larger house on the land in Boyce became vacant and Penn said that we could move into it. We needed the room and I would be closer to the stock and the feed for them was also in the barn near that house. Living in the bigger house was much easier and it was about this time that Penn decided to try to raise Holstein calves. There were no jobs in this small county and maybe we could make some money on this venture.

Molly, Terry, Deanna and I drove Penn's Travelall truck to Cleburne, where we picked up the calf Penn had bought on a pilot project. At three days old, the calf was a big baby at 80 pounds or more. Every morning at 7:00 a.m. Molly fixed the calf's bottle and we took turns feeding him until he decided that Molly was his mother. Cute—but something she wasn't ready for!

We continued taking care of the cattle for several weeks and during this time two calves were born. We named one, a little bull calf, "Jones" and the other a heifer calf, Deanna named "Susie." They became her only playmates. However, I wasn't making one red cent and the only help we received was from Madeline who, God knows, was carrying the burden of feeding my family.

On May 15 a decision had to be made. It was apparent that the calf project wasn't going to materialize and Penn was talking of selling some of the land and cattle. It looked as though Penn was having financial problems and I did not want to add to them. So, Molly and I talked and decided the best thing for us was to drive to Dallas and make arrangements to stay with someone and for me to try one more time (there's that song title). We talked to my mother, who said we could move in with her until I found a job and a place to live.

As we drove back to Boyce, we spoke of our apprehension about moving, but when we drove into the yard we knew it was the thing to do. The front door of the house was standing wide open. I knew what was gone even before I got out of the car. I was right. The 30-40 Krag rifle (the only one I had managed to hang onto), Terry's 30.30 Winchester, which he had received as a gift, his 410 shotgun, and the 12 gauge automatic shotgun Penn had loaned me were all missing. These were our only means of protection in this place so far in the country with no telephone or close neighbors. Now we had been stripped of that. Coincidence? Maybe. I was very uneasy and the sooner we got out of there, I felt, the better.

It took two days and two sleepless nights to arrange the move but we did it and were back in Dallas and staying with my mother. By this time my physical health was somewhat improved and my mental attitude was back to normal. This was due to the words of encouragement I had received from Madeline and others who had written to us over the past months to let me know that there were people in this country who cared. I was ready for any opposition from the Political Monster which ruled Dallas and even the very lives of those so-called Business and Civic leaders who did not have the guts to stand on their own two feet! As I thought over the past years, I was even amused that I, a man of limited education and no social position in this City of Purity, had struck fear into the hearts of its great leaders by just speaking to them on the street!

Although I had not worked steadily since my termination from the Dallas County Sheriff's Department, I did not forget my obligation as an American. Thus, when asked by certain critics of the Warren Report to help, I did what I could. Imagine the turmoil it will cause when and if the Dallas Police read this and find out I have copied and turned over to a certain editor several names, addresses and telephone numbers of people connected with the assassination of John F. Kennedy which were locked in the files of the Dallas Police Intelligence Division. Not to mention the files which were photostated and smuggled out of the Dallas County Mail under Bill Decker's nose (all after I left the Sheriff's Department). Even though I have not made any money in the past few years, I hope I was able to help those who have spent so much time investigating the assassination, who certainly haven't made any money either!

The last week of May, 1970 I got lucky. The ad in the newspaper read, "Wanted Dispatcher for temporary labor company". The Company was Peakload. I quickly made a call to the chief dispatcher, with whom I had worked previously, and found he was working sixteen hours every day. He was so happy to hear from me, because of his workload, that he offered to come and get me so that I could go to work that day. The company had a new office manager, Jim Morris. I went in immediately to apply—at the urging of the chief dispatcher, Bill Funderburke—and for an interview with Jim Morris, the manager. He was from Ft. Worth and knew more about the assassination and me than I would have preferred (from the questions he asked me concerning Bill Decker, Jim Garrison and others who had made the news). However, the office was in trouble as they had not been able to keep an evening dispatcher for more than three or four weeks at a time since I worked there in 1969.

With a word of caution as to my activities, Jim put me to work. This made Bill very happy as the pressure was now off him. I knew the work, the customers and most of the men I would be dealing with so Peakload did not have to worry about breaking in a new man. The rest of May and early June passed uneventfully but around the middle of June Molly went into Baylor Hospital, through the clinic as we could not afford a private doctor or the high rate of regular hospital services (I had only worked a short time and we still had a balance owing on Molly's surgery in August 1969). On June 26th, Molly underwent major surgery. She had been under a tremendous strain the past years and was physically and mentally exhausted.

During this period, I had managed to gather enough money to buy a 1962 Ford from a friend. It was not the best car in the world but it was only a hundred and fifty dollars and it did run. I paid $50.00 down and was to pay him the rest in a month or so. I also rented a small apartment and it seemed good to once again be by ourselves in our own home. But our new found Wealth was short lived.

Shortly after this, a self-professed private detective in Dallas, by the name of Al Chapman, had written a story about new evidence in the assassination which he had sold to the National Enquirer. In this article he quoted me as saying that I had given certain information to him and had personally identified a picture of a man and car saying it was Lee Harvey Oswald and his accomplice.

The entire story, with reference to me, was completely false. I had never been interviewed by this man and had at no time seen the picture to which he referred. Al Chapman, prior to the assassination, was a custodian for a church in Oak Cliff. There is a good deal of mystery about him for he will not reveal his business or residential address. Nor is the name of the church available. Although he is a part-time private investigator, he has no license.

The story was all over the office and Jim was concerned as he had been keeping up on anything written involving these events. Before long the

F.B.I. and the Dallas Police were making regular visits to the office on the pretext of looking for "Jim Jones" or "Tom Smith" or any excuse they could use to let me know they could also read! The heat was on. Jim was constantly there—every time I looked up—which was unusual. This leech, this skid row bum, and I am referring to Al Chapman, in his lust for money, not caring whom he hurt, had not only sold his story but my future with Peakload as well.

On July 17, 1970, I reported for work to find another man doing my job. I was told by this "replacement" that Jim wanted to see me. As I sat in Jim's office, I knew what was coming. Jim said, "Roger, you've done a good job but it is time for a change." I asked him for an explanation but all he would say was that it was time for a change and he was sorry!

Bill Decker died in August. The County Commissioners appointed his executive assistant, Clarence Jones, to fill the job until November, when he had to run for election (with the backing of the Democratic Party). For the first time since Decker's reign, the Republicans nominated someone to oppose a Democrat for the office. The man was Jack Revel, former Chief of the Dallas Police Intelligence Division. This meant that the voters had the choice between two evils. Well, Clarence Jones was elected—his campaign signs and posters read, "Elect Clarence Jones— In the Tradition of Bill Decker"! It would be nice if Jack Revel would be upset enough over his loss of the election to make public some information—but this is very wishful thinking indeed.

Meanwhile, I am still out of a job (but still looking). I would like to think that the people of Dallas will change and rise up against the dishonest and irresponsible tyrants who govern in their name—but I do not see it happening in the near future. Dallas is my home but I will always feel like an outsider because I simply will not adjust to the idea that for Dallas, for Texas, for America this must serve as democracy.

A Few Odd and Interesting Facts

Allen Sweatt, Decker's Chief criminal investigator, let me know that he was aware of my friendship with Hiram Ingram and that he did not like it one bit.

Before I departed the Sheriff's Office for good Allen Sweatt and I talked a couple of times and he revealed to me that he knew Lee Harvey Oswald. He also told me that Oswald worked for the F.B.I. as an informer, that he was paid $200.00 a month and his code number was S 172.

ROBERT PERRIN AND NANCY PERRIN RICH

When Penn Jones wanted the records of Robert Perrin, the ex-husband of Nancy Perrin Rich, I had to find a new source of information. (I won't release this name for obvious reasons.) It seems that Nancy Perrin was connected with Jack Ruby, Clay Shaw and Lee Oswald at about the time of President Kennedy's death.

Robert Perrin was reported to have committed suicide in New Orleans, La. The autopsy showed no visible scars, marks or tattoos and Penn knew that Perrin had been arrested in Dallas and wanted me to get the records of the arrest along with his description. After some doing I finally obtained the record. It showed that Perrin had several tattoos and part of his right index finger was missing. None of this information showed up on the autopsy report. It would be interesting to know who WAS buried in Robert Perrin's place and where Robert Perrin is now, wouldn't it?

ADDENDUM

The favorite pastime in Dallas

Is a game they call murder with malice

They don't ask your leave

But not to deceive

To tell you would be—well, too callous

CAR ACCIDENT

On Wednesday, October 27, 1970, I went to downtown Dallas to Jack Revel's campaign headquarters to pick up some campaign signs. The headquarters were not open and I decided to visit a friend who works at a restaurant across the street. While talking with my friend the conversation turned, as it so often does, to the assassination. He and I had discussed this in the past.

During the course of our conversation a man who I had not met before entered into the conversation. He, of course, did not know me (not to my knowledge). I told him that I was from out of town and that I was interested in facts that hadn't been printed and in persons that had known Jack Ruby and Lee Oswald. This man said, "I knew Oswald and Ruby. I can tell you anything you want to know about them."

At this point I became very interested and I told him again that I'd sure like to know firsthand what they were like. He said, "I knew Ruby well—I had seen Oswald a couple of times in Ruby's place." I then said, "Well, in Ruby's business—the night club—I imagine a lot of people were seen there." He sort of chuckled and said "Huh—Jack Ruby's business was spelled Mafia." He then said, "I can show you a used car lot where Ruby collected a lot of gambling money over on Ross Avenue" (it was the 4600 block of Ross Avenue). So I offered to drive him over there and he said, "No—do you have your car here?" I did. He said I should follow him, which I did. I parked my car on the same side of the street as the car lot, a short distance down and walked back to his car. I opened the door of his car on the passenger side and he pointed to the car lot and said, "That's where a lot of the money comes in from the gambling operation and Jack picked it up here."

He said, "If you really want to know what's going on in Dallas you have to talk to someone who's been around—and I've been around in those circles." Then he said, "Just leave your car parked there and come with me—I'll show you something that's REALLY interesting." He drove me to 300 1/2 South Ewing in the Oak Cliff area to an apartment that had been a family dwelling and was converted into apartment units. I should mention here that Jack Ruby's address at the time of the assassination was 323 South Ewing.

The apartment at 300 1/2 South Ewing is upstairs and when we walked into the apartment there was a distinct feeling of an unlived-in atmosphere. The furnishings were bare. There was a couch, chair and coffee table—no lamps, no ash trays, nothing on the walls. The man had been smoking so it was odd that there were no ash trays. He said, "How about a cup of coffee?" We went into the kitchen, he opened the cabinet and said, "Oh well, I guess I'm out of coffee." He was also out of everything else as there was nothing in the cabinet.

The arrangement of the apartment was unusual as you had to go through the bedroom to the kitchen, which was very small. The closet door was open in the bedroom. However, there were no clothes in it. At that time, I became slightly nervous about the situation.

We went back into the bedroom from the kitchen. While in the bedroom he said, "I want to show you something." He opened the top drawer of the dresser and pulled out a shoulder holster—there was a 32 revolver with a three-inch barrel in the shoulder holster. He pulled the 32 out of

the holster and said, "what do you think about that?" I remarked that you don't see many 32's with a barrel like that. He put the 32 back in the drawer and went around to the side of the closet which was not visible when you went into the kitchen. At that time, he produced two rifles— one was a bolt action which looked like a 30.06, the other was a high-power automatic which appeared to be a 257 caliber.

I remarked that they were nice rifles and I would like to have a good deer hunting rifle. He then laid those two on the bed and he said, "You haven't seen anything yet." He then got down on the floor and he pulled 5 more rifles from under the bed. Each of these were equipped with scopes. He then pulled a cardboard box about 13 inches long and 10 inches deep also from under the bed. The box was closed and on the side was printed "Ammunition—Handle With Care." He then slid the rifles and ammunition back under the bed. I said jokingly, "What are you gonna do—start a war?" He said, "Could be."

At that time, he looked at his watch and said "excuse me just a minute, I have to go down to the landlady's apartment and make a phone call—I promised some people I would call them" (there was no telephone in the apartment). He was gone for about ten minutes. During this time, I made a mental inventory of the apartment. After he returned, he asked me if I was ready to go back to my car. There was a pay phone on the corner from the apartment and I asked him to pull over so that I could call the people who owned the car (I had told him that it was borrowed while I was in Dallas), that I wanted to let them know that the car was okay. From the pay phone I called my wife and gave her the man's name and address and told her of the situation. His name—as he gave me is A.E. Allen, 300 1/2 South Ewing, Dallas, Texas.

Before we went to his apartment, or the apartment, I told him being from out of town that I didn't know much, but that I had heard that Ruby was in the gun running business. He said that Ruby wasn't actually buying and selling weapons. That people in higher positions made the arrangements for the buying and selling of weapons. That

Ruby was mainly the go-between for delivering the money and making arrangements for the storage of the weapons until they were shipped out.

During the course of the evening he made the statement several times that, "if you want to stay healthy, don't say anything to anybody in Dallas about the assassination unless you're damn sure you know who you're talking to."

He then said that there were a lot of people in Dallas who were out to "get" him because he knows too much.

One of the strangest things that he did was to drive on East Jefferson to a used car lot and stop. There were two men inside the office and he went in and talked to them. I stayed in the car and could see them through a window of the office. He was in there only a few minutes. His car was a light blue Oldsmobile 66 model. When he came out of the office, he got into a gray Olds sitting on the lot, and he drove it onto the drive stopping just before he entered the street—he motioned to me— I was watching him. I got out of the blue Olds, and he took me back to my car in the gray Olds.

On the way to my car across town, he kept repeating there's a lot more to this (the assassination) than they'll ever know. In taking me to my car he cut across to Ft. Worth Avenue. While driving slowly along he pointed out certain private clubs—saying that he wasn't allowed in one or the other. My first thought was that he was trying to give me the impression that he was knowledgeable about the workings of the Dallas underworld. However, it really seems that he was using a delaying measure—since it took from 10:00 p.m. until 11:15 p.m. to drive me to my car—an ordinary 15-minute drive at that time.

When I got out of his car at mine, he said, "I'll call you tomorrow." Earlier in the evening he had implied he was going to give me more information. I had given him a number to reach me by. Needless to say, I did not hear from him after the incident that followed!

I had locked my car when I parked it. When I got into it, I turned the key over to start the engine. At this point there was a muffled type explosion and then smoke came out the sides of the hood. The hood had a double latch and didn't blow. Fire was coming through the air vents under the dash and a pillow was burning inside the car.

I jumped out of the car and raised the hood. The engine, hoses, firewall and even under the bell housing was all ablaze. Several persons came up and someone called the fire department. A man named Bill Booken was walking by at about the time it happened. The fire department used 2 cans of chemical to extinguish the fire. This was one of the hottest fires I had ever seen. There was no smell of gasoline before or after, there was no back fire as the car had not started and afterwards the gas lines were checked and there were no leaks. There was an air breather on the car and in fact, there was no mechanical reason for the explosion.

This happened at 4625 Ross Avenue. Mr. Booken took me to Anderson's Restaurant at 4909 Ross Avenue where I called my wife and she arranged for my brother Duane to come after me. I didn't know that I had been injured until I felt the warm blood running down my shirt after my brother picked me up. I had lost quite a lot of blood by the time I went to the emergency room. I was there for three hours. A police report was made. I had received 5 puncture type wounds in the chest area. One vein had been severed and had to be tied and stitches taken in the wounds. X-rays were also made. I went to our family physician the following day and had the stitches removed the following Monday. It was never completely determined what hit me. Another close call! The doctor at the emergency room said I was lucky the wounds had not been lower and our family physician said I was lucky the wounds were not in the neck. So . . . I suppose I'm just lucky all the way round!

"I believe in my country. I have done nothing but tell the truth, and I will continue to do so."

—*Roger Dean Craig*

May 12, 1936 – May 15, 1975

ADDITIONAL READING

THE DEPUTY INTERVIEWS:
THE TRUE STORY OF J.F.K. ASSASSINATION WITNESS, AND FORMER DALLAS DEPUTY SHERIFF, ROGER DEAN CRAIG
by Steve Cameron (Author), David Ratcliffe (Foreword), Phil Singer (Preface)

The Deputy Interviews: The True Story of J.F.K. Assassination Witness, and Former Dallas Deputy Sheriff, Roger Dean Craig, written by author and researcher Steve Cameron, is a book of interviews conducted with JFK assassination experts, insiders, & family members who knew former Dallas Deputy Sheriff Roger Dean Craig, who witnessed numerous events that occurred in Dealey Plaza on November 22, 1963, that dramatically contradict the Warren Commission's final conclusions about the J.F.K. assassination.

Publisher: Steve Cameron Productions
Language: English
Paperback: 316 pages
stevecameronproductions.com

ALSO AVAILABLE

THE PATIENT IS DYING: ADAPTED FROM ROGER CRAIG'S 1971 MANUSCRIPT "WHEN THEY KILL A PRESIDENT"
by Roger D. Craig (Author), J. Gary Shaw (Foreword), Donald Jeffries (Preface), Rita Musgrove (Introduction), Robert J. Groden (Afterword)

Steve Cameron's new companion piece to his groundbreaking book *The Deputy Interviews*. *The Patient Is Dying* includes new material, including a foreword written by first generation JFK assassination researcher and author, J. Gary Shaw (*Cover-up, JFK: Conspiracy of Silence, Trauma Room One*), a preface written by best-selling author Donald Jeffries (*Survival of the Richest, Hidden History, Bullyocracy*), and an afterword written by world-renowned JFK assassination researcher and author, Robert J. Groden (*JFK: The Case For Conspiracy, The Killing of a President, JFK: Absoluteproof*).

Publisher: Steve Cameron Productions
Language: English
Paperback: 122 pages
stevecameronproductions.com